Why do we eat?

Stephanie Turnbull
Designed by Zöe Wray
Illustrated by Tim Haggerty

Nutrition consultant: Dr. Kristina Routh
Reading consultant: Alison Kelly,
Roehampton University

Contents

A busy body

Your body is like a machine. It needs fuel to keep going.

Food is your fuel. It gives you energy to move and think.

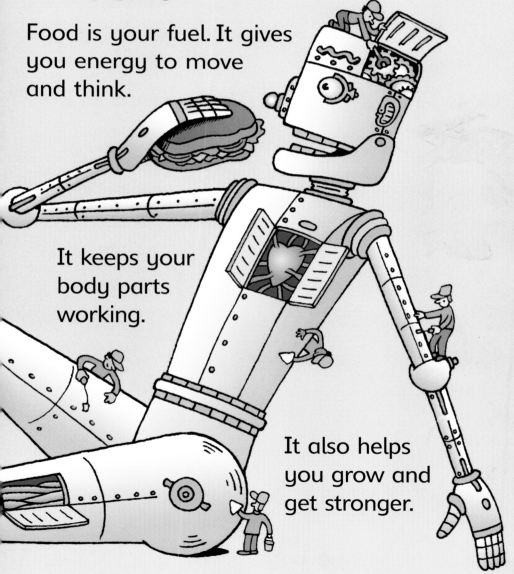

It keeps your body parts working.

It also helps you grow and get stronger.

In your mouth

You need to process your food before it can be used to keep your body going.

Your teeth chop and grind food into small pieces.

Your tongue pushes food around.

A juice called saliva makes food soft and easy to swallow.

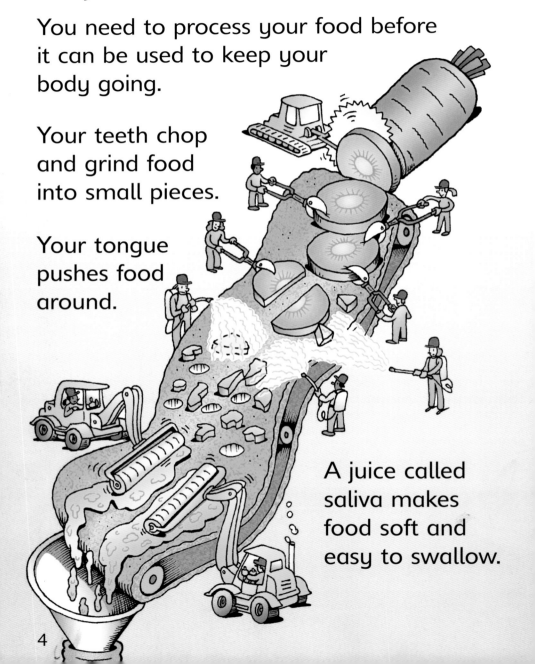

When you're hungry, your mouth makes lots of saliva - even before you've eaten anything!

Food goes down a tube called the gullet when you swallow.

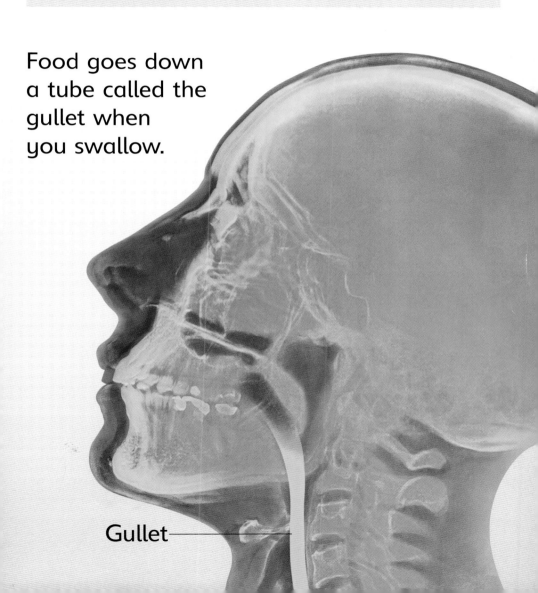

Gullet

Food factory

After you swallow, the food goes down into a stretchy bag called the stomach.

The food is mixed into a thick mush inside the stomach.

The mixture moves into a curly tube called the small intestine.

Useful chemicals called nutrients are taken out.

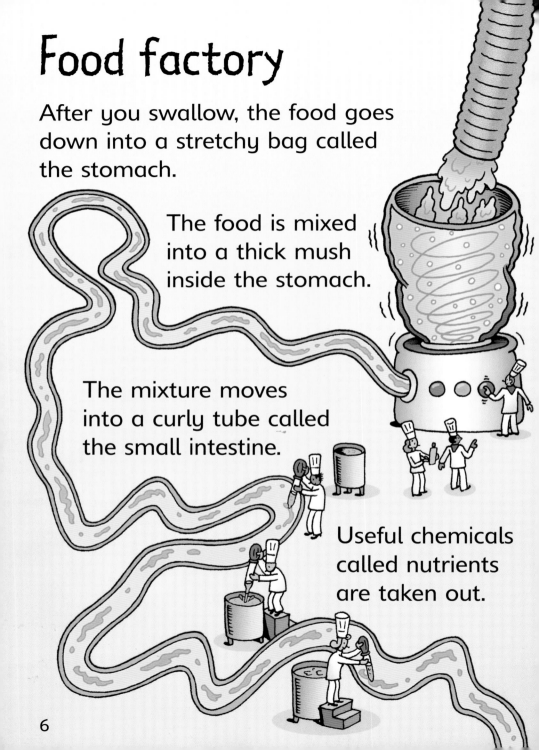

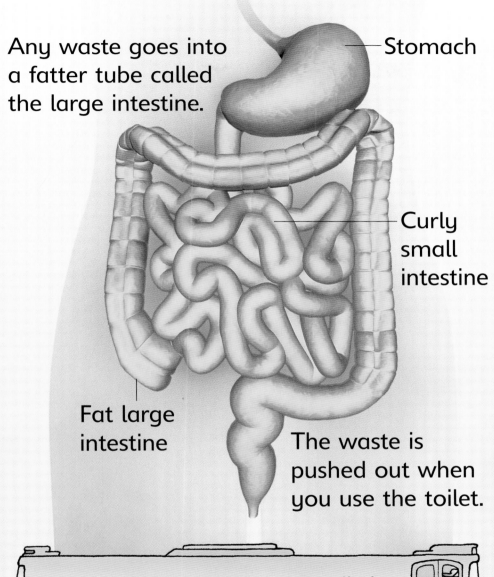

Any waste goes into a fatter tube called the large intestine.

Stomach

Curly small intestine

Fat large intestine

The waste is pushed out when you use the toilet.

If your small intestine was uncoiled, it would be about as long as a bus.

Nutrients

Food contains three main things that your body needs - proteins, carbohydrates and fats. These are all nutrients.

Proteins come from meat, fish, eggs, milk, cheese, nuts and beans.

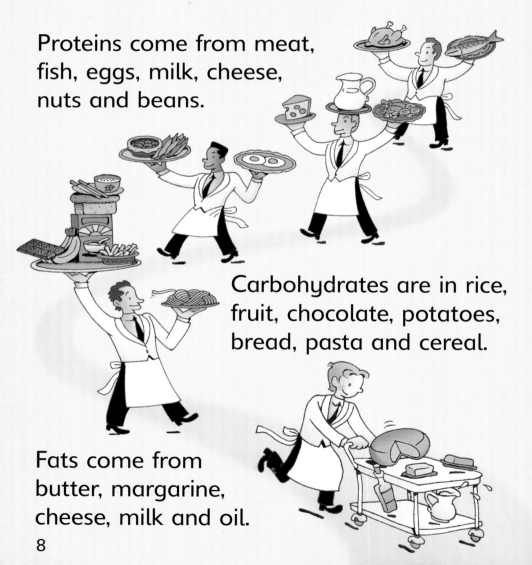

Carbohydrates are in rice, fruit, chocolate, potatoes, bread, pasta and cereal.

Fats come from butter, margarine, cheese, milk and oil.

Proteins, carbohydrates and fats from the food you eat are taken to your liver.

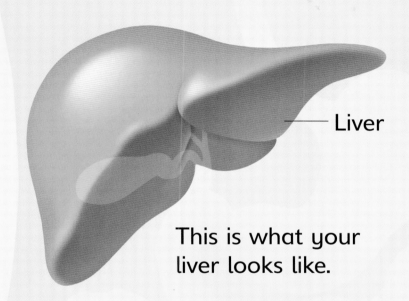

Liver

This is what your liver looks like.

The liver sends the nutrients to all the different parts of your body.

Nutrients travel to and from the liver in blood.

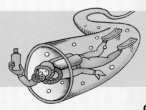

Proteins

Unlike machines, your body can use its fuel to grow and get stronger. Your body needs proteins for this.

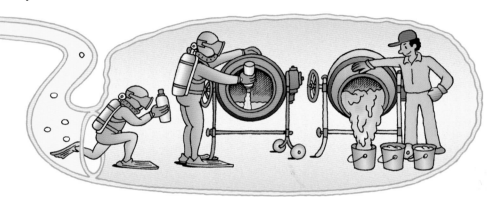

Proteins are turned into useful materials inside the liver.

These materials build up different parts of your body, such as skin and hair.

Your fingernails and toenails are also made from proteins.

Many thin layers of proteins make up your skin and hair. You can see some of the layers in this magnified photograph.

Skin ──────── Hair

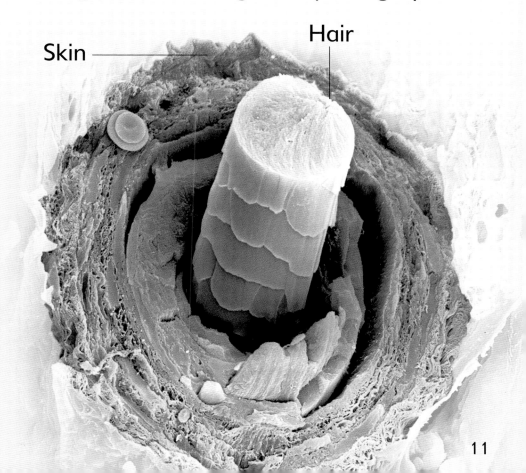

Carbohydrates

There are two types of carbohydrates - starch and sugar. They keep your body going, just like fuel keeps a car going.

Foods such as bread and pasta contain starch.

Sugar comes from sweet things such as chocolate.

Starch gives you energy that lasts for a long time.

People who need lots of energy eat plenty of starchy foods.

Sugar gives you a quick burst of energy...

...but it doesn't last for very long.

Fats

Fats give you extra energy. If your body doesn't need this energy right now, it is stored in tiny cells.

Fat cells are stored all around your body, underneath your skin.

If you eat too much, there is a lot more fat to store. This can make you overweight.

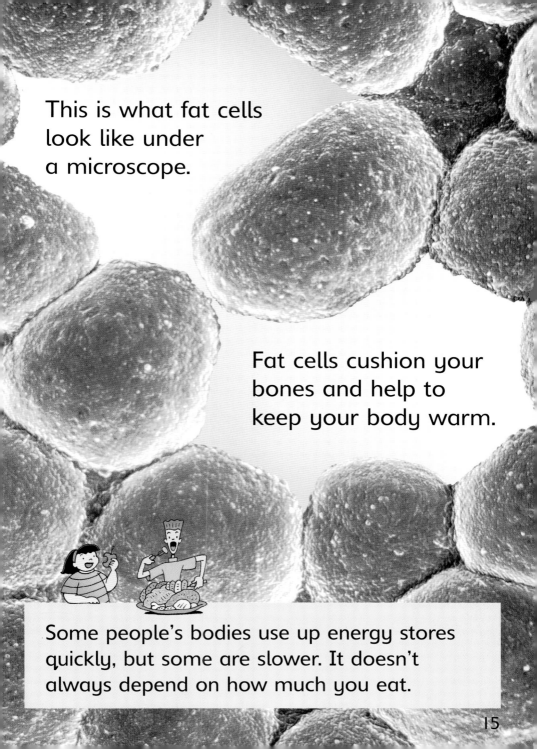

This is what fat cells look like under a microscope.

Fat cells cushion your bones and help to keep your body warm.

Some people's bodies use up energy stores quickly, but some are slower. It doesn't always depend on how much you eat.

Vitamins

Vitamins are extra nutrients that keep you healthy. Many foods contain vitamins.

Vitamin A helps you to grow and see in the dark.

Vitamin B gives you extra energy to be active.

Vitamin C helps your body heal itself and makes muscles grow.

Vitamin D makes your bones and teeth strong and healthy.

This is what healthy
bones look like.

Your body
makes some
Vitamin D itself,
using sunlight.

Without Vitamin D,
your bones would
be soft and weak.

They would bend
and break easily.

Minerals

Your body also needs small amounts of extra nutrients called minerals.

1. Minerals are tiny grains that come from the ground.

2. Plants that grow in soil take in some of these minerals.

3. If you eat the plants, minerals get into your body.

4. The minerals help keep your body working properly.

Calcium is a mineral that is found in green vegetables. Eating plenty of calcium helps your bones to stay strong.

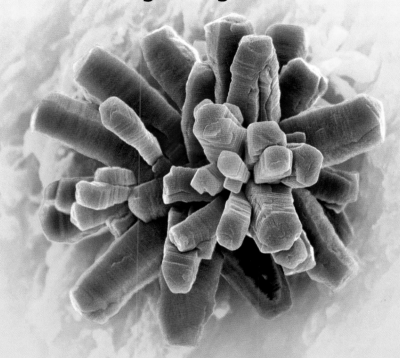

This is what a grain of calcium looks like under a very powerful microscope.

Salt is a mineral. Your body needs salt, but too much can be bad for you.

Water

You can drink water on its own, but there is also water in fruit, vegetables and in all drinks.

Water goes into your small intestine and helps move food along.

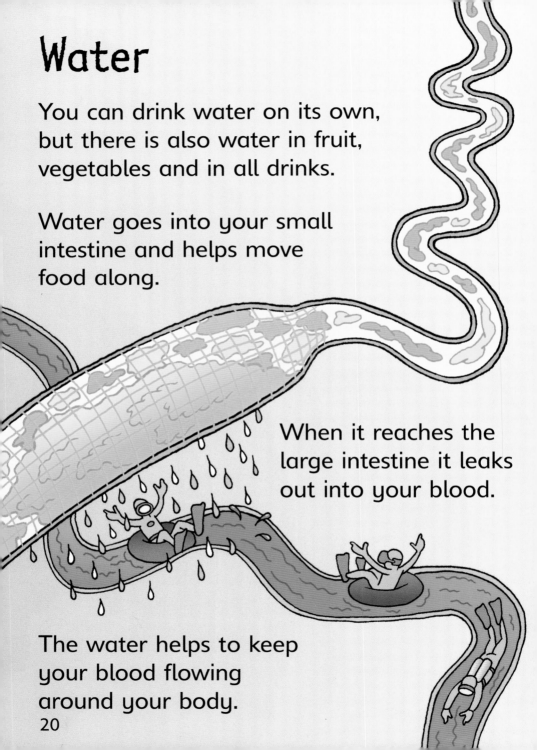

When it reaches the large intestine it leaks out into your blood.

The water helps to keep your blood flowing around your body.

When you are hot, water is pumped out onto your skin as sweat. This helps you cool down.

Extra water goes into two bean-shaped parts of your body called kidneys.

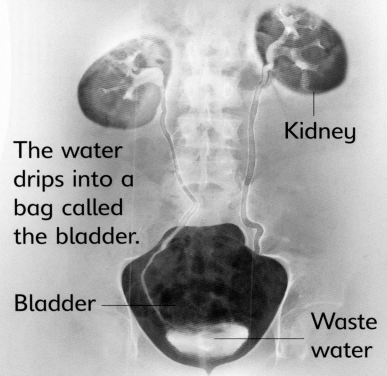

Kidney

The water drips into a bag called the bladder.

Bladder

Waste water

Waste water comes out of your body as pee when you use the toilet.

A load of junk

"Junk food" is the name given to food that contains a lot of fat or sugar. A lot of junk food is fried in lots of oil. This can make it very fatty.

It is unhealthy to eat too much junk food.

A can of cola contains up to ten teaspoons of sugar!

Sweet foods and drinks leave a sticky coating on and between your teeth.

Over time, this makes your teeth rot and fall out.

You can help to keep your teeth healthy by brushing them twice a day.

Smart eating

Eating a good balance of different foods will help you to stay healthy.

You need to eat more fresh fruit and vegetables than any other foods.

Your body also needs plenty of energy foods such as bread, pasta and cereal.

Exercising also helps to keep you healthy.

Smaller amounts of meat, fish, milk and cheese give you the proteins you need to grow and get stronger.

Vegetarians can get proteins from beans and nuts.

You shouldn't eat too many fatty or sugary foods.

Food poisoning

Tiny things called germs live all around us.
Some of them can cause food poisoning.

1. Germs can live on food. They spread by splitting in two.

2. After a short time the food may be covered in germs.

3. If you eat the food, germs attack your small intestine.

4. Your body pushes the food back out, making you sick.

26

 You can stop germs from spreading by cooking food or keeping it cold.

Sometimes germs from your hands get into your mouth and make you sick, too.

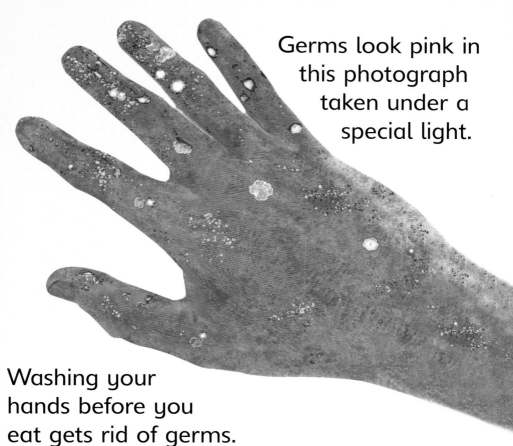

Germs look pink in this photograph taken under a special light.

Washing your hands before you eat gets rid of germs.

Food allergies

Your body can make a mistake and think that a certain food is a dangerous germ. This is called a food allergy.

Foods such as nuts and strawberries often cause food allergies.

Your body zaps the food with a chemical called histamine.

Histamine can give you itchy skin and a runny nose, or make you sick.

28

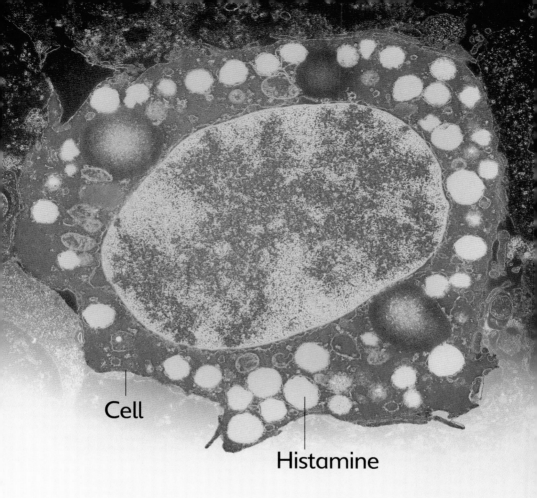

Cell

Histamine

The pink spots in this magnified photograph are histamine. They come from cells in your blood that fight germs.

You can have allergies to other things too, such as pollen from flowers.

Glossary of food words

Here are some of the words in this book you might not know. This page tells you what they mean.

 saliva - Liquid in your mouth that makes food soft and easy to swallow.

 nutrient - A chemical in food that your body needs to keep working.

 starch - A type of carbohydrate in foods such as bread, cereal and pasta.

 cell - A tiny part of your body. Some cells contain droplets of fat.

 vegetarian - Someone who doesn't like to eat meat or fish.

 germ - A tiny living thing that can get into your body and make you sick.

 histamine - A chemical that your body makes to help fight germs.

Websites to visit

You can visit exciting websites to find out more about food and eating.

To visit these websites, go to the Usborne Quicklinks Website at **www.usborne-quicklinks.com** Read the internet safety guidelines, and then type the keywords "**beginners eat**".

The websites are regularly reviewed and the links in Usborne Quicklinks are updated. However, Usborne Publishing is not responsible, and does not accept liability, for the content or availability of any website other than its own. We recommend that children are supervised while on the internet.

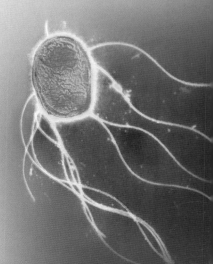

This is what a germ looks like under a powerful microscope.

Index

Acknowledgements

Photographic manipulation by John Russell
With thanks to Catriona Clarke

Photo credits

The publishers are grateful to the following for permission to reproduce material:
© **Alamy** 9 (John W. Karapelou, CMI), 17 (Friedrich Saurer), 22 (Pictor);
© **Science Photo Library** 5 (CNRI), 7, 27 (Alfred Pasieka), 11, 19 (Steve Gschmeissner),
15 (ISM), 21 (Du Cane Medical Imaging Ltd), 29, 31.

Sun, moon and stars

Farm animals

Elizabeth I

Rubbish & Recycling

Dogs

Horses and ponies

Spiders

Planes

Cats

Ancient Greeks

VOLCANOES

DINOSAURS

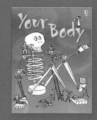
Your Body

Armour

Sharks

The Celts

VIKINGS

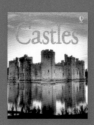
Castles

How flowers grow

Digging up the past

Living in space

Caterpillars and Butterflies

Ballet

Pirates

EGYPTIANS

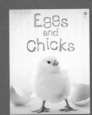
Eggs and Chicks

ROMANS

Weather

Tadpoles and frogs

Why do we eat?

Under the sea

Bears

AZTECS

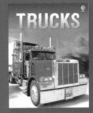
TRUCKS

Night Animals

Firefighters

Antarctica

Bugs

COWBOYS

Planet Earth

London

Seashore

China

Dangerous Animals

Rainforests

Trees

Reptiles

Ships

Bats

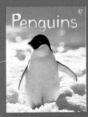
Penguins